GW00514650

NORTH HARROW LIBRARY
429-433 PINNER ROAD
NORTH HARROW
HARROW HA1 4HN

1 3 APR 2013

0 7 MAY 2013

Row ark

i

Other Easy Step-by-Step Guides by Brian Brown include:

Motivating your Staff for Better Performance

Managing Change

Better Budgeting for your Business

Easy Step Guides by Pauline Rowson include

Marketing

Successful Selling

Telemarketing, Cold Calling & Appointment Making

Building a Positive Media Profile

Being Positive and Staying Positive

Communicating with More Confidence

Fundraising for Your School

Easy Step Guides by Brian Lomas include

Giving Confident Presentations

Stress and Time Management

Fewer, Shorter Better Meetings

Negotiating for Success

Also available:

Writing Advertising Copy

Writing Newsletters and Articles

Recruiting the Right Staff

Handling Confrontation

enquiries@rowmark.co.uk

www.rowmark.co.uk

Easy Step by Step Guide

Writing a
Business Plan
and Making it Work

Brian B. Brown

NORTH HARROW LIBRARY
429-433 PINNER ROAD
NORTH HARROW
HARROW HA1 4HN
TEL: 020 8427 0611

658.
401
brow

2 7 JUN 2006

Rowmark

First published in 2006 by Rowmark Limited

65 Rogers Mead
Hayling Island
Hampshire
PO11 0PL

ISBN 0–9548045–1–1

© Brian B. Brown 2006

The right of Brian Brown to be identified as the author of this work
has been asserted by him in accordance with the Copyright, Design
and Patents Act 1988.

All rights reserved. No part of this publication may be reproduced
in any material form (including photocopying or storing it in any
medium by electronic means and whether or not transiently or
incidentally to some other use of publication) without the written
permission of the copyright owner except in accordance with the
provisions of the Copyright, Designs and Patents Act 1988 or under
the terms of a licence issued by the Copyright Licensing Agency
Ltd. 90 Tottenham Court Road, London, England W1P 9HE.
Applications for the copyright owner's written permission to
reproduce any part of this publication should be addressed to the
publisher.

Warning: The doing of an unauthorised act in relation to a copyright
work may result in both a civil claim for damages and criminal
prosecution.

Note: The material contained in this book is set out in good faith
for general guidance and no liability can be accepted for loss or
expense incurred as a result of relying in particular circumstances
on statements made in this book.

Edited and typeset by
Frances Hackeson Freelance Publishing Services, Brinscall, Lancs
Printed in Great Britain by
RPM Reprographics Ltd, Chichester

Contents

About the author

After a 'first career' during which he held senior general management and executive positions in the engineering, manufacturing and financial services industries, in 1987 Brian became a freelance consultant working with large and small organisations, from private to public sectors, to improve organisation performance through strategic change and training.

Brian is a business graduate, Chartered Secretary, and member of the Chartered Institute for Personnel and Development. He also is a visiting lecturer at the University of Southampton.

Introduction

Why should you use your valuable time creating a document that tries to look into the future while the world is changing around you? How can you decide now what you will be doing in one year's time, or three years' time, or even five year's time? And, if you can't predict these things, what value would a plan have anyway?

The usual, perhaps trite, answer to these questions is, if you don't know where you are going, how will you know when you get there?

But there is far more than that to business planning, and particularly in making your business plan work. Whether you are a business owner, or a manager, you will know that doing business is a complex operation. It is a matter of trying to juggle a number of different factors, and arranging for those factors to be in the right place at the right time.

Creating a business plan means not only identifying all the factors in your area of operation, it also means developing a deep understanding of each of those factors individually, and the way they combine to create your unique business situation.

How to use this guide

This guide is written in a clear step by step style to make it as helpful as possible to you. I recommend that you read it through from beginning to end and then dip into it to refresh your memory. The boxes in each chapter contain tips to help you. Also at the end of each chapter is a handy summary of the points covered.

A good approach to your reading might be for you to consider the issues raised in this book and how they might be used beneficially for *your* organisation, rather than try to apply any technique in exactly the same way as the examples provided here. To this end I have included places where you might like to pause in your reading and consider the implications for your area of responsibility – these places are highlighted with a large question mark and are usually accompanied by a question you might like to consider. In fact, this is a good time to start how we mean to continue, to get you involved in creating a meaningful business plan:

> **?** What are the specific business factors that are important to you right now? What are the issues that you feel need to be covered by your business plan? Write down your feelings and ideas.

In response to this question you may have written things such as:

- I'm not sure how my products fit into the market place

- I would like to know what my competitors are doing

- will my bankers lend me more money for expansion?

The 'stop and think' questions through this book will help you to answer these, and many more questions about your business. The guidelines that I develop through the book will also show you how to make it 'work for you'.

If you are in any further doubt about the need for business planning, then imagine preparing a complex meal without a recipe, or assembling some complex equipment without an instruction manual. What both of these documents do is to:

- make sure you have all the things you need to do the job

- give you confidence that it has all been thought through

- provide a schedule to make sure you get things in the correct order

- identify points in the process when difficulties can occur

- help you to visualise what the finished product will look like.

Having a recipe does not mean that you must follow

it exactly. You can change according to circumstances, or what ingredients are available.

You can also customise it to suit your preferences and circumstances. This is also true of business planning.

What you will learn from this guide

By the time you reach the end of this book, you will have prepared a sound plan for your business. In the future, you may change some factors, or adapt it to the current circumstances. However, you will know so much about your business that you should never again be caught without an answer to where you are going, and what you expect to have when you get there!

> It is not a sin when things do not go according to plan.
>
> *It is a sin not to know* when things are not working to plan.

You will know exactly why, and how, you are changing your plan and that knowledge will give you confidence in the validity of your decisions.

What this guide covers

This guide is primarily concerned with how to create a business plan for your business or department, in the most effective way for your organisation.

It is also about making sure that your business plan is well designed to give you an effective blueprint for sound business management, and that by using that blueprint your plan will work!

Throughout this book, when the word 'products' is used it is also intended to represent your services if you are a service provider, or your raison d'être if you are a non-profit organisation.

What you will learn from this guide:

- what goes into a business plan
- where to get the information needed for your plan
- how each business factor complements and reinforces the other factors in the plan
- how a plan can be presented for external uses
- how to monitor and manage your plan
- what to do when things change
- how to extend your plan for a longer period.

Business planning, of necessity, covers every part of your business, and as you go through this book you will see references to other books in the Easy Step by Step Guide series.

These books have been brought to your attention to provide that extra, more detailed advice that will increase the successful implementation of a business planning process.

1

What is a plan and what does it contain?

A plan, according to the dictionary, is 'a diagram made by projection ... showing the relative position of parts ... way of proceeding ... scheme arranged before-hand'.

So, a plan is a document we are producing now, explaining a projected future by detailing the relative position of different parts or factors, and how those parts are used to proceed towards the planned future.

> A business plan is a schedule of factors brought together to create a desired future

So, from now on, you will be writing down, in a meaningful order, factors that are relevant to your business aspirations.

Where do we start? Let's get into the recording mode straight away – here comes that question again:

? What are the specific business factors that are important to you right now? What are the factors that you feel should be covered by your business plan? Write down your feelings and ideas.

As I said earlier, what you have written down is specific to you, and to your business circumstances. Whatever the pressures applying to your business at the moment, you should have included the following factors in your list:

- **Products** (remember this includes services) – are they right for the marketplace? Is there something I can do to make them better? Is the price correct?

- **Marketplace** – what is happening to my product? Am I in the right marketplace? What are my competitors doing? Who are my best customers?

- **Distribution** – how long does it take to get my products to market? What is my level of damage through delivery? Is my packaging attractive?

- **People** – do I have the right people in the right jobs? Will I need more people in the near future? Do I need to introduce training for my people?

- **Finance** – am I working to the correct budgets? Are my prices correct, or could I get more for my products? Should I be expanding the business?

- **Administration** – do I have everything under control? Do I pay, and get paid, on time? What happens to my business if I am ill? Do I need a successor, or should I be thinking about selling my business?

The factors listed above represent broad headings and you may have listed specific and more detailed questions related to these broad issues. If so, that is good, the more you are thinking now, the easier it becomes as we progress.

What these factors do suggest is that running a business generally focuses on a few, very important processes.

> **?** The above factors relate to business owners, looking at the whole business. If you are a departmental manager, are the business factors that you wrote down for the last question different? Will you need to look at all the factors, or just one or two? Write down your feelings and ideas.

In fact, in larger organisations, each of the processes detailed above is likely to be managed as a separate function.

However, if you are a functional manager in a large organisation, and are reading this book from the point of view of planning for a functional department, you will still need to consider each of the factors listed above. From a departmental point of view your list should probably include the following:

- **Products** – (this is the process for which your department is responsible, though it may not be a tangible 'product', that contributes to the organisation's product or service) – are they doing their job effectively? Is there something I can do to make them better? Is my contribution cost effective?

- **Marketplace** – how does my product contribute? Could I be offering services to additional departments? What are similar departments in other organisations doing better than me? What are my customers' needs? Could my department be out-sourced more effectively?

- **Distribution** – how long does it take to circulate my products? Is my packaging effective for the people using my products?

- **People** – do I have the right people in the right jobs? Will I need more people in the near future? Do I need to introduce training for my people?

- **Finance** – are my budgets effective and am I working to the correct budgets? Are my costs competitive, or could I be more efficient? Will I need additional finance in the foreseeable future?

- **Administration** – do I have everything under control? What happens to my department if I am ill? Do I need to be training a successor?

I will expand these ideas in the following chapters. However, there is one further factor that we need to drive our business plan (a factor which you may have listed in your original answer). That factor is **direction**.

We need to know where we are going, what our aspirations are, and how the process factors we have already identified will combine and contribute to a successful outcome. Because this is so important, it is the beginning of our voyage of discovery, and the content of the next chapter.

Example for TDC

Through the following chapters, I will use the example of TDC, a training and development company, to illustrate the business planning process.

TDC have the following products:

- pre-designed training programmes, with CD tutorials, sold by mail and internet

- customised training courses commissioned by corporate clients

- face-to-face training courses delivered for corporate clients.of TDC, a training and development company, to illustrate the business planning process.

In summary

Through this chapter I have introduced the following:

- a business plan is a schedule of factors brought together to create a desired future

- the main factors, for most organisations, that need to be covered by a business plan, are:
  products and services
  marketplace
  distribution and packaging
  people
  finance
  administration

- all of these factors are applicable both to an organisation as a whole, and to a functional department

- all of these factors combine, and contribute to the drive to achieve the outcome to which we aspire.

2

Where are we now?

Well, of course you know where you are now! You are dealing every day with where you are now, so you are clearly in the best position to answer this question. But can you answer the question objectively, or would you answer it by listing the problems you have to deal with today?

What you need to do is to try to adopt what can be a rather difficult position for some managers, called the *Helicopter Perception*. To do this, you must rise above the day-to-day issues that surround you and look down on the entire landscape of the business. Then, try to identify all the good factors and the not-so-good factors that make up your organisation.

You may be surprised by the amount of information that you have listed and the issues that you have forgotten about among the pressures of day-to-day management.

You may also find that some of the issues you have listed appear on more than one list.

? Imagine that you have been asked to show an important Government Minister around your organisation. Make the following list:

- all the good things that you would want to tell him or her about

- all the things with which you are uncomfortable and would avoid mentioning

- all the things that are outside your control and you would want the Minister to know about.

In order to maximise the usefulness of your list, we need to formalise the way in which it has been formulated, both to clarify the issues and also to make sure that you haven't forgotten anything. A good way of doing this is to arrange your list in the form of a SWOT analysis. This analysis creates an objective 'here and now' picture of your organisation and the major issues facing it currently and for the foreseeable future.

SWOT analysis

A **SWOT analysis** is an analysis of your organisation under the headings:

Strengths

Weaknesses

Opportunities

Threats.

A SWOT analysis is simply carried out by listing the characteristics of your organisation under each of the headings, usually by having a separate page for each heading.

However, there are a few guidelines that will help you create a more effective analysis:

- Strengths and Weaknesses should be 'here and now' while Opportunities and Threats will occur sometime in the future

- Strengths and Weaknesses usually relate to internal processes in the organisation, whereas Opportunities and Threats usually arise from outside the organisation

- Opportunities and Threats will include issues outside your control, such as changes in government policy, consumer fashion, and technological advances

- When you write down a factor under any heading you must consider whether it should *also* appear under a different heading. For example, a good sales manager may be a strength, but might also represent a threat of being poached by a competitor.

You have probably realised that a good SWOT analysis will provide you with the following objective information:

- factors (strengths) that are present in the organisation that will help you to achieve your aims

- problem issues (weaknesses) present in your organisation that you will need to address in order to achieve your aims

- events happening outside your organisation (opportunities) that could help you to achieve your aims and improve and grow your business
- potential events outside your organisation (threats) that could cause you problems in the future and could prevent you from achieving your aims.

Therefore, the objective information contained in a SWOT analysis will be invaluable to your business plan.

Taking into account the guidelines given above, the SWOT analysis for TDC is as follows:

Example for TDC

Strengths
- Positive business growth for the past 5 years
- Well-established product range
- Good reputation in the marketplace
- Number of 'blue-chip' customers
- All products aligned to government criteria
- Trained and loyal staff
- Good market identity (brand)
- Sales Manager best in the industry
- Positive bank manager support

Weaknesses
- Ineffective Internet web-site

- Well-established product range beginning to look boring
- Trained and loyal staff don't like new innovations
- Market identity (brand) is solid 'old-fashioned'

Opportunities

- Build on the positive business growth and stable finances for the past 5 years
- Update and develop established product range
- Use good reputation in the marketplace to launch new products
- Increase the number of 'blue-chip' customers
- Involve trained and loyal staff in new plans
- Enhance and update market identity (brand)
- Promote Sales Manager to drive new plans
- Include positive bank manager in the planning process
- Update and improve web-site

Threats

- Competitors' product ranges improving
- Faulty products could mar reputation
- 'Blue-chip' customers could defect to competition or train in-house
- Government criteria for training could change
- Loyal staff might create barriers to new changes
- Sales Manager could be poached by a competitor
- Bank manager could change

You can see that this sort of analysis provides a very useful insight into an organisation.

SWOT analysis is used extensively by managers in many major organisations, many of whom keep an organisation analysis in their organiser for continual reference.

I am also aware of organisations that continually refer to SWOT analyses through management and board meetings to remind them of the issues faced by the organisation.

? Go back to your list and transfer the items to four sheets of paper headed **strengths, weaknesses, opportunities** and **threats**.

Now, add to your list by carrying out a SWOT analysis for your organisation or department. Be honest and conscientious in detailing all the issues facing you. This information will be invaluable for developing your business plan.

In summary

Through this chapter I have introduced the following:

- the need to understand objectively where you are now

- the need to be aware of the good things present in your organisation that will help you achieve your aims

- the need to be aware of the things that you need to address now in order to achieve your aims in the future

- the need to identify the opportunities that might present themselves in the future

- the need to be aware of threats that could hold you back in the future

- the relevance of a SWOT analysis

- how to design a SWOT analysis for your organisation.

3

Where are we going?

You cannot produce a business plan showing your intended future actions unless you know what you aim to achieve during that period.

The following diagram illustrates this dilemma:

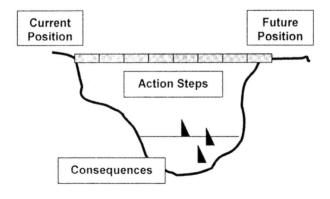

The process illustrated in this diagram is the movement from where you are now, to where you want to be – that is, the 'sun, moon and stars' of your aspirations.

The **action steps** are what need to be put into place to enable you to bridge the gap between the present and the future.

The **consequences** are the result of you failing to effectively plan your action steps, or leaving a gap in the bridge. This leaves you vulnerable to falling into the shark-infested waters below!

You have probably realised that action steps are another name for the business plan, but before we can consider what your action steps should be, we need to look at the relationship between where you are now, and where you want to be in the future.

You have already objectively identified where you are now through the SWOT analysis you carried out in chapter 2. In particular, the elements of your SWOT analysis represent the following factors in the above diagram:

- **strengths** are action steps, or planks in the bridge, that are already in place

- **weaknesses** are gaps in the action steps or bridge planks that need to be addressed to prevent you falling through to the sharks

- **opportunities** are the future position that you can achieve providing you can get across the bridge

- **threats** are the shark consequences of failing to address weaknesses or take into account adverse external influences.

What we now need is a similar exercise to identify

where we want to get to!

You cannot hope to achieve your future aspirations unless you know what you are aiming for. At an overall organisational level this means knowing what the organisation (the sum of all its resources) expects to achieve over a given time period – that is, its aims or objectives.

> **?** Does your organisation have a set of overall objectives, possibly called its Mission and Goals? If so, get hold of a copy, or write them down for yourself.
>
> If you do not have a set of overall objectives for your organisation, or department, write down now, in your own words, what you want to achieve in the future.

Objectives can be described in different management jargon but invariably add up to the same thing – a series of value statements about the organisation, often comprising one or more of the following:

- **vision** – a long-term visualisation of what the organisation will look like in the future
- **mission** – what the organisation expects to achieve in the long term
- **goals/aims** – specific factors to be achieved in the short term
- **objectives** – significant, measurable actions necessary to achieve the stated goals
- **values** – standards of behaviour that should be

observed when actioning objectives.

Since every person in an organisation must share in, and contribute to the achievement of the organisation's Mission and Goals, it is important that they are written in language that is memorable, easily understood and kept to a minimum. This then makes it an easy task for employees at every level to continually remind themselves of the targets and issues for which they are personally responsible.

> **?** Go back to your organisation goals and read them through again. Would you say that they are memorable, written in straightforward language and short enough for everyone in the organisation to remember? If you are not sure, it might be a good idea to ask several employees to tell you what they think the organisation's goals are. Can you think of ways that the goals can be amended to make them simpler and more memorable? Write down your ideas.

Some organisations have laborious 'Mission & Goals' statements, which are forgotten almost as quickly as they are written. The more complex the organisation the more likely it is to have a long statement, though it can be argued that this should not be necessary. Memorable statements are often very short phrases or even single words – for example:

"No surprises" (international hotel group). This phrase, which every employee could repeat without any hesitation, came from the fact that employees could only give the best performance if they knew what was going on – in other words, that no one would be surprised by good things or bad things happening every day. By communicating everything and immediately dealing with identified weaknesses, the 'no surprises' objective was achieved.

"Enthuse – develop – support – deliver" (training organisation). In this organisation, it was recognised that success would be achieved if staff and customers were enthused by the organisation's products and service; if staff and customers were involved in developing and delivering the right products; if excellent support was provided to staff and customers alike; and if delivery of the final product was excellent.

? Can you think of a short phrase to embrace your organisation philosophy?

To be effective, organisation objectives need to be:

- **objective** – clearly identifiable in terms of what you require to be done

- **measurable** – written so that you will be able to measure performance against them – ie. what will be completed by what date

- **achievable** -   set at a level that stretches the organisation and its staff but that you know can be achieved

- **agreed** – by all the people who have to achieve them

- **monitored** – regularly by you.

If you would like an easy way to remember these

characteristics, use the **'SMART'** mnemonic:

Specific
Measurable
Achievable
Realistic
Time focused.

A balanced view of objectives

Looking at the objectives you have written down so far, you may find that they are intermingled, rather than identifiable in the neat sections mentioned above.

To create a clear planning process, you should try to create 'balanced' objectives across all the drivers rather than rely on objectives couched only in financial or statistical terms. A goal such as 'achieve a ten percent increase in sales by the end of the year' might be good to aim at but does it ignore the effect it might have on customers and staff in the long-term? Is it possible that your sales team might achieve the ten percent increase in sales by offering unprofitable deals? Or might they pressurise customers for additional orders to the point where you lose good customers?

Areas such as customer satisfaction, organisation systems, development of new products or services etc. may not have goals that are absolutely objective. However, to ensure the success of your business plan, it is important that you are able to identify the really vital factors, without which the organisation has little chance of success in the long term.

In many business plans, the following factors are often overlooked, but are ones that can have a great impact on the successful achievement of the plan (though you may want to add other areas for your organisation):

Customer satisfaction – the ability to deliver an enhanced level of products and services to current and potential customers.

Organisation development – the ability to learn continually from your experiences so as to create an ongoing competitive advantage.

People optimisation – the ability to attract, keep and develop the right people who can continually deliver excellent performance.

Organisation processes – the ability and willingness to change and manage the organisation's processes and systems to support, to a high level, all other factors.

Financial ability – the ability to achieve financial targets, and to satisfy the needs of the current business and its investors (if any).

? When you wrote down your objectives earlier, did you take into account the areas detailed above? If you think that this way of thinking might be helpful to your organisation, would it be useful for you to group your objectives under these headings? Once you have done so, are there any gaps that need to be addressed?

If you complete this exercise, you have probably begun the blueprint for successful change in your organisation!*

---

* More information and guidelines on designing objectives can be found in the Easy Step by Step Guide to Motivating Your Staff.

This process will help you to focus on those measures critical to your organisation's future, and force you to consider all the operational aspects that you will need to include in your business plan.

Let's have a look at how our example organisation, TDC, has designed its objectives. You will see that its long-term 'mission' is supported by short-term goals that meet the SMART criteria, and that it has a value statement that drives the organisation ethically.

Example for TDC

TDC intends to expand the business over the next three years and has set the following criteria:

Our mission is to have doubled our business in the next three years, putting us in the top five in our industry by that time.

Our goals are to:
- increase our annual turnover by 30%
- maintain our net profitability at 15% of turnover
- increase customer satisfaction by reducing the number of customer complaints by 10% per annum
- maintain staff turnover at no more than 3% per annum.

In pursuing our business interests we will always treat our staff and our customers ethically, and will not discriminate against anyone except to employ staff on the basis of ability and suitability for the job.

> **?** Now re-visit your objectives and make sure you have objectives that are:
>
> **S**pecific
> **M**easurable
> **A**chievable
> **R**ealistic
> **T**ime focused.

Now, you not only know where you are coming from, but also where you want to get to.

In summary

Through this chapter I have introduced the following:

- a diagrammatic view of business planning showing the present position, future aspirations, action steps and the consequences of failing

- how the SWOT analysis from chapter 2 fits into the business planning diagram

- the need to have objective and realistic aims for the future

- the importance of an effective Mission and Goals statement

- how to design SMART goals.

4

What about our products?

In order to be successful, you must have the right products (or services), at the right price, in the right place, at the right time.

This is easy for me to put down in words, but I am very aware that it is much more difficult to achieve on the ground. However, the statement itself suggests some important questions that we need to address as we develop our business plan. These questions are:

- Are our products right for the current market?

- Is the marketplace likely to change in the future and will our products be suitable for the new marketplace?

- How do our products compare with those of our competitors, both in terms of quality and of price?

- Does our current pricing structure give us the profit margins we need for future development?

- How does our service compare with that of our competitors?

- Do we have the best distribution and sales systems, and how do they compare with our competitors?

> **?** Look back at your SWOT analysis and identify factors that you wrote down that relate to your products or services. Do you have any major product weaknesses that need to be addressed? Have you identified any future threats to your product range?

Although you may have listed various observations about your products, the only people who can truly tell you how good your products are, now and for the future, are your customers. This means that in order to get an objective view of your products, you need to talk with your customers, or potential customers, directly or indirectly.

Talking with customers, or potential customers is called market research.

Market research

You might think that market research is something that only large organisations do. Certainly, many large organisations employ market researchers to try to answer the questions posed above.

However, it is not necessary to employ an agency, or outside people in order to carry out some market research. This is something you can do yourself, providing that you have the time to devote to it. Be warned that market research can take time!

Getting information means asking questions, so the

first thing to do is decide the questions you need to ask in order to get the information you want.

> **?** List the questions you need to ask about your business.

You should have included the following questions in your list:

1 Do you recognise the name (or logo) of our products?

2 How do you know about our products? (Advertising, recommendation, gift)

3 How often do you buy our products? (Daily, weekly, monthly, annually)

4 When did you last buy one of our products? (in the last week, month, quarter, year)

5 Did that product meet your needs?

6 What was the best thing about the product you bought?

7 What was the worst thing about the product you bought?

8 How could the product be improved to meet your needs?

9 Why do you choose to buy our products? (Price, quality, fashion, practicality)

10 Why do you choose not to buy our products? (Price, quality, fashion, practicality)

11 If our product was improved to meet your needs, what percentage increase in price would be

acceptable to you for the improvement? (5%, 10%, 15%, 25%, 50%, more than 50%)

12 Do you find it easy or difficult to locate our products? (Very easy, fairly easy, not very easy, difficult, very difficult)

13 Would you recommend our products to someone else? (Yes, no, perhaps)

You may want to include questions for specific issues such as packaging, instructions, ease of operation, quality of customer service, and many others.

Note that I have included a range of answers, in brackets, for some of the questions. Having a set range of answers means that you can have a questionnaire with tick-boxes, and that makes it easier to make an assessment of the information from a number of completed questionnaires. It also makes it easier and quicker for the customer to answer.

How many questionnaires do you need to get a meaningful amount of information? The answer to that is, as many as possible, because the more information you have, the more accurate it is likely to be. However, your market research must also be aimed at the range of people that might use your product.

For example, if you make baby products, there is little point targeting the over-60's for market research information; and if you provide public services, there is little point targeting children (unless you are asking about play facilities).

Also, if your potential customer base covers a wide range of different people, you must make sure that you get responses to your questionnaire from across the entire range. If you are marketing kitchen utensils, your range could include different people within the following groupings:

- age (under 20, 21–35, 36–50, 50–65, over 65)
- status (single women, single men, married couples, single mums, single dads, parents)
- ethnic origin
- wealth (earnings level, type of residence, home location).

This information would give you a fairly clear idea of the group of people that are more likely to buy your products, and therefore the group of people to whom you should direct your selling and promotional activities in the future.

However, as suggested above, you must have a number of completed questionnaires from each of the relevant groups for it to be meaningful. One hundred questionnaires, all from white women in their twenties would tell you very little about who buys your kitchen utensils. Similarly, one hundred mixed questionnaires with only one single mum, one over-sixty and one Asian man would not give you a clear picture of your potential customer base.*

It is also a good idea to try to spread your market research activities between different days of the week, and perhaps over several weeks. In this way you avoid the possibility of getting too many people of a similar type (Tuesday shoppers may be different types from Friday or Saturday shoppers).

Once you have obtained a number of completed questionnaires across a good spread of potential customers, you will probably be able to extract the following information:

- How well-known is your product (Question 1)?

- What form of promotion gives the best results (Question 2)?

- What is the buying pattern for your products (Questions 3 and 4)?

- How good is the product in the customers' eyes (Questions 5–10)?

- How could your product be improved (Question 8)?

- How much can you viably spend to improve the product (Question 11)?

- How good are your sales and distribution channels (Question 12)?

- How loyal are your existing customers (Question 13)?

> **?** Go back to the list of questions you wrote down earlier, and formulate them into a market research questionnaire that you can use to gather information, or to instruct an outside agency.

Once you have received adequate responses to your questions, you should have a good picture of your product, your customers, your advertising and what your customers expect in the future.

---

* For more information on all aspects of marketing, see The Easy Step Guide to Marketing.

All of this information has a bearing on your SWOT analysis (which you might now like to update with the new information) and ultimately on your plans for the future.

Let's look at how TDC, our example organisation, might deal with market research.

Example for TDC

TDC intends to expand the business over the next three years but needs to know if its current products are acceptable to current and future customers. TDC decides to carry out its own market research by targeting existing customers and other organisations that it has identified as potential customers. TDC has a good reputation and maintains close relationships with in-house training managers. Therefore, TDC considers that it should be possible to get those training managers to complete a questionnaire; in response TDC offers one of their background music CD's free for each completed questionnaire received. (This will be much less expensive than commissioning an outside agency to do the market research.)

The TDC questionnaire will focus on:

- existing customer satisfaction with the products

- product changes that customers might want to see in the future

- new products that customers are looking for

- what may encourage new customers to buy the existing, or new products

- the quality of selling and promotional activities.

Because TDC consider their staff to be a vital part of their product, they also intend to conduct a staff survey to get the staff's views about the products and about working for the company.

In summary

In this chapter we have considered how you can become more aware of your product and your customer base.

To get the required level of information, you need to carry out market research for which you need the following:

- a questionnaire listing questions for all the information you want

- a profile of the range of people that are existing or potential customers for your product

- the time to carry out the market research, or the financial ability to engage an outside agency to carry out the market research for you.

Your market research must aim to show how closely your products fit the business need to have 'the right products, at the right price, in the right place at the right time'.

5

Customers and competitors

Everyone has customers. If you don't have customers, you don't have a job or a business. This is because every commercial activity, whether in the private sector or the public sector, is aimed at providing a product or service to an end-user – the customer.

> **?** Your market research should have given you a sound idea about your potential customer base – that is, the range of people likely to be your customers. Go to your market research information and list your likely customer characteristics. If you have not yet completed your market research, list what you believe to be your customers' characteristics.

You have probably listed a number of characteristics such as age, gender, status and wealth factor, and this is a good base from which to begin. Another factor, which you may not have analysed from your market research, is the level of loyalty you can expect from your customers.

Customer risk factors and loyalty factors

If you think about your own spending patterns and those of people close to you, you may realise that we are all different in our approach to what we buy. For example, we all display different risk profiles, so our buying pattern will differ between the following types:

- those who never take risks and always buy products they know or preferably have tried before

- those who always want the latest innovation, or the latest product advertised on television, irrespective of price.

Coupled with the **risk factor** is the **loyalty factor**.

The loyalty factor represents the probability that a buyer will choose your products or services for the next similar purchase.

I should point out that, if you are working in the public sector, these customer distinctions still apply to you even if your customers have no choice about dealing with you. However, where customers are forced into a monopoly situation and cannot choose their suppliers, their level of satisfaction becomes a level of dissatisfaction.

Because all customers are different in their approach to purchasing, and a public service does not provide a range of choices to meet those different characteristics, the lack of choice for customers means that their perception of your service always starts from a point of dissatisfaction. Extreme bureaucracy in public services means that the management of those services will probably dissatisfy most of the people, most of the time.

Commercially, however, customers have choices. Will they buy the same product again, or will they choose to buy a different product? Again, people tend to fall into categories of buying behaviour such as the following:

- those who always buy the same product or brand irrespective of price or advertising. However, if the preferred product is not available, these customers may choose an alternative and become loyal to the alternative

- those who buy according to price or advertising. That is, those people who respond to promotional offers

- those who buy 'randomly', probably according to design, or packaging, or perhaps even according to retail positioning. In this group are the 'reverse price conscious' customers who always buy the most expensive choice because 'more expensive must mean better quality'.

> **?** Do you have a feel for the buying characteristics of your customers, perhaps from the market research information? List your perceptions of the risk tolerance and buying behaviour of your customers.

The buying characteristics of your customers are important when we look at promotional activities in chapter 6. An analysis of customers' buying characteristics for our example organisation, TDC, shows the following:

Example for TDC

Customer Risk Profile

Existing customers display a low risk behaviour because training programmes are designed in conjunction with the customer and customers only undertake a risk level acceptable to them. However, selling to new customers, particularly via the internet, is likely to attract higher-risk customers who want to use latest technology to deliver training. *Therefore, TDC will need to ensure that it has the relevant expertise and skills to be able to address new customer requirements.*

In terms of loyalty, existing customers remain loyal to TDC because of the close relationship built up during the design and delivery stages. For existing customers, TDC is often the only provider they contact because the company understands their needs and has a proven ability to meet those needs. This will not apply to new customers who buy according to specification and price when compared with other suppliers. *Therefore, it will be necessary for TDC to increase its promotional activities for new customers as a means of updating information on technical merit. It may also be necessary to discount some products to compete in the broader marketplace.*

Clearly, it is important to know your customers' buying behaviour if you are not going to lose them to your competitors. It would also be useful to know what your competitors are doing, and just how great a threat they pose.

Competitors

Finding out what your competitors are doing is another of those activities that larger organisations contract out to independent agencies. However, it is also something that you can cover yourself to some extent if you have the time to do so.

> **?** Make a list of your major competitors, and the advantages that you think they might have over you.

It is sometimes said that products or services are sold according to quality or price. That is, customers will accept a low quality for a low price, or will pay a high price for high quality. Unless you produce throw-away fun products, or hand-made high-value products, this axiom no longer applies. Customers now expect a minimum, relatively good quality of product for which they also expect to pay a price at a level that is 'value for money'.

Therefore, you cannot accept that your products or services are sold purely on the basis of low price. Price, quality and value need to be balanced in order to achieve customer loyalty.

> **?** Go back to your competitor list. Have you noted that any competitor has a price or quality advantage? If so, look at that competitor again to determine what that advantage means – is it a price advantage, or a quality advantage, or does the competitor have a more balanced offering?

> **?** This is also a good time to go back to your own product analysis and decide whether your products or services are of a higher quality than the customer needs, and whether your price level needs to be adjusted up or down to provide that 'value for money' balance.

Competitor research

You can get information about your competitors from a number of different sources, such as:

- the market research questionnaire

- observation of competitor activities

- publications produced by competitors. For example, sales leaflets, marketing brochures, and annual report and account documents.

In addition, market information, including information about competitors, can be obtained from data stored at most public libraries. Check the information available in the reference section of the library – a good reference is usually a publication called Mintel (an acronym for Market Intelligence) that carries reports for a wide range of market categories. Mintel is also available through the internet.

The information for which you are looking should aim to answer the following questions:

- Who are my major competitors?

- Are competitor products aimed at the same market

segment as mine?

- How do competitor products compare with mine in terms of ability, quality and price?

- Is any competitor planning a major change in marketing strategy?

- How do competitor expenditures for promotional activities, and research and development, compare with mine?

- Are competitors optimistic or pessimistic about the future marketplace?

Competitor research for our example organisation, TDC, provides information shown below.

Example for TDC

Mintel has provided the following information:

- TDC is the seventh largest provider of customised training packages in the UK.

- TDC's turnover of £1.8m is 16% of the industry market value of £11.25m.

- Mintel expects the training market to grow by at least 12% per annum for the next five years.

- It would be possible for TDC to move up to become the fifth largest provider in five years time based on a comparison of products.

The largest three providers in this industry are associated with major IT companies and get much of their business through the parent companies. Products for these suppliers are of good quality, average price but not very innovative. However, they are unlikely to be challenged in the short-term.

Other industry products are in a similar category to TDC current products. There is no evidence that challengable competitors intend to carry out any major changes to their products or price levels, which are comparable to TDC. *The opportunity is therefore present for TDC to introduce new, innovative products at viable price levels, while remaining aware that competitors may offer lower prices on existing products while they try to catch up with our new products.*

Clearly, it is important to know your customers

In summary

In this chapter, we have continued to look at the 'planks' that need to be put in place in order to achieve our future objectives. In particular, we have considered the following:

- how we can objectively analyse our existing and future customer base so that we can try to provide products or services that best meet customers' needs*

- how we can get information about our competitors

- how the information we collect can lead us to the data that needs to be taken into account in our future business plans.

---

* More information about marketing can be found in the Easy Step by Step Guide to Marketing.

Business is about selling or marketing products or services at a profit. Therefore, the business planning process must take into account the processes that make up the business chain.

The final part of the marketing/selling function in this chain is promoting the product. This is the subject of the next chapter.

6

Promoting the business and selling the products

> **?** List the ways in which you promote your business and sell your products.

Internal promotional activities*

To a large extent, promotional activities need the support of external organisations for things like advertising, design and printing. However, there are also promotional activities that you can carry out internally.* These internal activities include the following:

- regular contact with customers, and potential customers, either through representative visits or telephone updates

---

* More detailed information on these activities can be found in the Easy Step by Step Guides to Successful Selling, Telemarketing, Cold Calling and Appointment Making.

- mailing customers to update product information
- inviting customers and potential customers to promotional events
- developing appropriate advertising for your products and image
- involving customers in product development.*

Some organisations use media coverage as a positive promotional activity and maintain regular contact with media representatives such as newspaper reporters, industry magazine editors and, occasionally, television news-desks. For these organisations, it is important that positive information is fed regularly to the most appropriate media outlets.**

External promotional activities

As mentioned above, most promotional activities involve the support of external organisations. You should have discovered from your research the ways in which your customers get to know about you – through some form of advertising, recommendation, leaflet distribution or perhaps through your internal promotion activities.

You should also be aware, from your competitor research, how your competitors promote their products.

---

* More information about internal promotion is provided in The Easy Step by Step Guide to Writing Advertising Copy, and Writing Articles and Newsletters.

** More information on media management is provided in the Easy Step by Step Guide to Building a Positive Media Profile.

Therefore, you should already know what works best for you currently, and what processes will help you to achieve your future objectives. Issues that you need to take into account are:

- loyal customers generally require less advertising to maintain their loyalty

- high-risk customers need more promotional activities to keep them informed of new product innovations

- price-conscious customers need more advertising in the form of leaflets and offers

- random customers usually choose products in proportion to the volume of advertising and the attraction of packaging.

Therefore, developing and maintaining a customer base that is loyal, and continues to buy your products, is a worthwhile and cost-conscious strategy.

Where you get involved in advertising, make sure that your advertising is clearly focused on the customers you want to attract. It is a well-known fact that a 'scattergun' approach is rarely cost-effective and often results in one-off customer purchases. That means you have to advertise again to get more customers.

Targeted advertising is aimed at specific customers, or a specific group of potential customers that are likely to become loyal to your products and therefore need less advertising maintenance in the future.

The advice therefore is to clearly identify the customer base that you want to attract, and use the appropriate promotional activity to target that base as exactly as possible. This is cost-effective promotion!

Distribution

All the promotion in the world will not achieve anything if the customer cannot access your product or service.

Imagine your reaction if you saw a newspaper advertisement for an offer that you found attractive, but then could not find an outlet where you could buy the product. The advertising would be wasted, and the producing organisation would probably have lost the opportunity to make you a loyal customer.

So, make sure that your distribution channels display the following characteristics:

- they are open, not only for sales but also for the receipt of new deliveries

- there is an efficient re-ordering system in place

- your supply process is fast and efficient – there is little point in you spending money on advertising if you cannot supply the products in the time required by customers

- your outlets display your products effectively to attract customer attention

- outlet staff have clear and updated information about your products and particularly about any offers available

- you monitor distribution outlets regularly

- sales outlets have an input into any changes you intend to make in the future.

? Go back to your list of promotion and selling activities. Do they meet the criteria given above for the following:

- targeted promotions
- regular contact with, and updating of customers
- regular monitoring of sales outlets
- efficient ordering and supply systems
- involvement of your own and sales-outlet staff in marketing decisions.

If you are in any doubt about the positivity of your answers, write down the actions that you will need to take to improve the effectiveness of your advertising and distribution.

Example for TDC

Promotion

TDC has traditionally promoted its products by specific advertising in personnel magazines and by a presence at personnel exhibitions.

TDC maintains a careful check on its advertising expenditure and any direct sales resulting (but accepts that there can be a lead-time of several months between initial customer contact and the receipt of an order). In the past trading year, TDC have experienced the following results from advertising:

Advertising Spend (£):	*New Customer Contacts:*	*New Business Income (£):*
Personnel Today magazine		
16,500	39	198,700
Management Today magazine		
9,000	3	14,300
Director magazine		
12,000	1	1,300
Personnel and HR Exhibition		
63,800	23	212,600

Sales and Distribution

A substantial proportion of TDC's sales comes from direct contact with customers by following up leads generated by promotional activities. TDC does not have dedicated sales personnel and customer contact is made by TDC trainers, or programme designers according to customer needs. The trainer or programme designer who is allocated to best meet the customer's requirements is responsible for maintaining ongoing customer contact, and is paid a small bonus percentage of the customer's annual orders.

The above system has worked well for TDC in the past, but *TDC recognises the need for a significant internet presence and plans to employ a specialist to design and continually update an effective website.*

TDC intends to review its promotional activities for the coming year.

In summary

In this chapter, I have outlined the issues that you need to look at regarding your promotional activities. These issues include the following:

- the need for targeted advertising aimed at attracting loyal customers

- the realisation that the random purchase customer costs more to maintain, both through the need for repeated advertising and special offers, and because of the extra cost of special packaging

- the need to involve your own employees, and those of your sales outlets in marketing decisions that might affect them and the way they work

- the importance of efficient sales outlets

- having an effective supply system to support those sales outlets

- the need to review your current marketing and sales procedures, in a similar way to that shown in the TDC example

- the need to identify actions that you need to take in order to achieve the objectives that you decided earlier.

7

People

In chapter 6, I talked about the need to involve employees and people from sales outlets in marketing decisions that could affect their way of working. Also, I mentioned the possibility of involving customers in discussions about major changes and new products.

There are a number of reasons for involving as many people as possible in business decisions.*

which are:

- people who are involved in the day-to-day contact with customers, or with others in the supply chain, will probably have much clearer perceptions of business operations and the things that could be done better

- people are more likely to embrace changes if they are involved in the decisions from which those changes result

---

* More detailed information on involving people in business decisions is provided in the Easy Step by Step Guide to Motivating Your Staff.

- involvement encourages motivation and motivated people do a better job
- you will gain a much broader view of the business from people you involve.

So, involving people in the decision-making process, and perhaps sharing with them your objectives for the business, is a good idea! But, how do you make sure you have the right people in the first place?

However good your objectives, and your products, and your promotional activities, it is often the employees that can make or break an organisation's reputation. How many times, as a prospective customer, have you felt irritated or angry when faced with a surly, uncooperative or downright rude individual? How many times have you taken your business to another supplier as a result of poor service? Yet the organisation you were trying to deal with probably had their positive objectives and their carefully engineered marketing plans.

? Go back to your objectives and look at them again in relation to your current staff. Do you think that your current staff can deliver your future business objectives? List your positive assessments of your staff, and your negative assessments of your staff. Were these points included in your SWOT analysis? They should have been!

Let's be clear about the issues here – the points that you have listed above, both positive and negative are the result of staff characteristics and your decisions.

You cannot blame an individual if you made an incorrect decision when you put them into their job!

However, making decisions about other people is notoriously difficult, particularly during interviews when people try to present their strengths and suppress their weaknesses. So, we need a strategy for getting and keeping the right people in our organisations.

Getting the right people

> **?** Think about the last time that you engaged a new employee. What processes did you adopt for advertising the job, short-listing the applicants and interviewing the possibles?

Many organisations use a specific employee job description from which an advertisement is produced, or perhaps repeat the advertisement that was used when the job was previously vacant. Both of these options assume that the organisation is static and has not moved on since the job was previously vacant. In this case, you may well be advertising for the person you needed months or years ago, rather than the person you need today.

The search for a new or replacement employee is the opportunity to analyse your specific current requirements. Therefore, you should ignore any previous job description, and particularly ignore any previous job advertising, and define *exactly* the job you *need* to be done, and the type of person you *now* need to do that job. Also, if you have a personnel department responsible for staff appointments, do not allow them to do anything until you have completed the suggested analyses – remember that your personnel department probably has different objectives from you, that is to fill the vacancy.

It would not be unusual for a manager to tell me that she or he does not have time to do these analyses. My answer is always the same – you do not have the time **not** to do them unless you want the risk of the wrong person in the job and the damage that he or she may have done. Remember your experiences as a customer!

Getting the right person in a job means that you have to get it right in the beginning, so make sure you know the type of person you want and that your job advertising reflects your needs. The questions you need to ask yourself will probably include the following:

- What qualifications does the job need?

- What qualifications would be good to have for the future development of either the business or the individual in the organisation?

- Are there any personal characteristics that an applicant *must* have in order to do the job?

- What experience is *necessary* for this job?

- Does the job involve unsocial hours with which applicants would need to comply?

- Does the job involve travel away from home, or overnight stays away from home?

- Do we expect the applicant to live within a specific distance from the workplace?

- What are the growth opportunities in this job?
- What career advancement does this job offer to the applicant?
- Are there specific applicant characteristics that would be unacceptable to the organisation (e.g. smoking in a medical environment)?

We are all used to seeing job advertisements with lines and lines of description, yet you can see from the above questions that the actual requirement for most jobs comes down to relatively few questions.

Therefore, having decided the *necessary* characteristics for the vacant job, you are now able to define the person you need and prepare a meaningful job advertisement.

You can also design a profile of requirements that you can use at interviews to collect all the relevant details that you will need to make a decision between the short-listed applicants.

By the way, I have heard of employers, and particularly personnel departments that are faced with an overwhelming number of applicants, who use very questionable methods of short-listing. These include rejecting applications on the 'wrong' size or colour of notepaper, rejecting applications that are not word-processed, and short-listing every seventh application in a large batch!

None of these methods is acceptable to you! If you have designed the job advertisement objectively, the applications should all be reasonably well-focused. Also, because you have an applicant profile, you should go through *every* application and only reject those that do not meet the *necessary* requirements of the job. There is no correct number for short-listed applicants and if your objective is to get the best person for the job, then you must take the time to do that irrespective of the number of applicants you interview. Professional golf coaches have a saying, 'Pay me now, or pay me later' because they know that poor action now will get reinforced to the point where it will take more attention to sort out in the future. The same applies to you and to applicant interviews – get it right now or pay for it later!*

This also applies to interviewing, incidentally, because there is only one person who will recognise the most suitable applicant for your team. That person is you, and for this reason you should not allow an appointment to be made for your team except by you.

I have mentioned the ability to prepare an interview profile from the job and person analyses that you carry out for any new or replacement job. This profile is a list of the characteristics that you will look for in every applicant. I use a separate profile sheet for each job applicant, both as a question reminder of the information I need from each person, and as a measure of each applicant's responses.

For example, I usually prepare a profile form that can have the applicant's name at the top, and displays the relevant questions as a left-hand column. I then add more columns as follows:

- a 'tick' column to show that the applicant meets *necessary* criteria such as a specific level of qualification

- a 'desirable' column in which I note characteristics

---

* More detailed information on recruiting techniques is provided in the Easy Step by Step Guide to Recruiting the Right Staff.

that I would *like* to have in the successful applicant but which are not absolutely necessary

- a blank column in which I can write my observations as the interview proceeds

- a 'score' column in which I can write a score (perhaps out of ten) that I perceive the applicant to have achieved for each question. The overall score can be useful for making a judgement between two equally good applicants, but I would not use it as the only means of deciding which applicant to appoint.

My profile forms also have a space at the bottom in which I can write my overall impressions immediately after each interview. This enables me to review all of the interviews at a later date in order to decide the best applicant to appoint. Some interviewers also request a photograph to attach to each profile form as an additional means of identification.

As you have probably realised, the entire appointment process detailed above is extremely objective and is aimed at getting the right person in the right job in order to meet the objectives you have set for your future business plan. This process also significantly reduces the possibility of choosing an incorrect applicant for the wrong reasons.

Keeping the right people

Having attracted the right people into the right jobs in your organisation, it is extremely frustrating to find that a member of your staff has been poached by another organisation. Not only have you lost an effective member of your team, but you are also now involved in the time-consuming and expensive process of finding a replacement. The cost of losing a key member of staff is significant and includes:

- your time to analyse the job and design relevant advertising
- the cost of advertising
- the adverse effect on the business related to the loss of the key person
- your time for interviewing and deciding on the appropriate applicant
- the cost of training the new person
- the ongoing adverse business effects until a new person is appointed and has achieved an equal performance to the person who has left.

The total sum of these costs alone is a very good reason to keep good people in your organisation. Every individual has his or her reasons for staying in any place and you should be close enough to your team to be able to answer the following questions for each member:

- What motivated this individual to join my team?
- Has anything changed since she or he joined?
- Has the person or his/her circumstances changed since (s)he joined?
- What are this individual's needs from his/her job?
- Are we addressing those needs?
- Would this individual benefit from training?
- When did I last talk with this individual about his/her personal aspirations?

- What is this individual's career plan?
- How can I help this individual to meet his/her career plan?

The secret of keeping good people therefore comes down to the following:

- knowing each individual in your team and understanding each person's motivation
- staying close to, and having regular discussions with each person
- having an agreed career plan in place for each person
- arranging training and personal development activities to meet the individual's aspiration for growth and job promotion.

You may be surprised that there is no mention of money, or performance payments as a means of keeping good people. My assumption is that you are already paying salaries in line with, or slightly above market levels.

Therefore, personal growth and job promotion opportunities are likely to be far more important than money to motivated people – performance payments often cause more problems than they solve.* Good training and a clear promotion path, in an enjoyable working environment, are more likely to encourage key staff to remain with your organisation.

In turn, those retained staff will be vital to your achieving the objectives you set as part of your business plan.

---

* For more information on performance payments, see the Easy Step by Step Guide to Motivating Your Staff.

Example for TDC

TDC has always had a policy of employing and keeping the right staff and have included this strategy in the organisation's objectives.

As trainers, we understand the motivational benefits of providing training and development opportunities for all our staff. We do not offer performance payments generally, though we do pay a small commission, based on account turnover, to employees responsible for specific customer accounts. Our intention was to encourage key staff to stay close to their customers and, from this point of view it has worked. However, it has also caused dissension among support staff who feel that they also play an important part in retaining customer business. *Therefore, TDC may have to review this performance payment in the future.*

TDC will also have to appoint an additional member of staff to design and manage the new website, plus additional training of designers to support the electronic training side of the business. We are currently reviewing the training designer job description and will put together a job profile from which job advertisements will be decided.

In summary

Achieving your business objectives has a great deal to do with people.

In this chapter, we looked at the need to attract the right people into the right jobs for which you should apply the following:

- take the opportunity to review job descriptions when a new or replacement member of staff is appointed

- make sure that a previous job description is updated to reflect the fact that the organisation has moved on and the old job description no longer covers the organisation's needs

- use a job profile to focus attention on the *necessary* requirements of the job rather than the 'nice-to-have' factors

- take the time and effort to appoint the correct applicant first time and not incur the high costs of staff replacement in the short-term

- keep key people in the organisation by focusing on knowing each person's motivation

- provide the growth, development and job promotion factors that will probably be more important to key employees than performance-related payments.

8

Finance

As the saying goes, 'Money is the root of all evil' and from a business point of view it is money, or probably the lack of money that causes the most major problems.

So, the final plank in our business plan will have to reflect the importance of adequately financing the future aspirations of the business.

Money from sales

The best finance will come from your own efforts, not only because that is the purpose of your business but also because being financially successful is very motivational for everyone involved.

Money from sales is not just the result of selling an appropriate volume of products. It is also the result of properly deciding the price at which you sell those products. This decision usually arises from the process of costing your products, mostly using a system of Total Absorption Costing.

Total Absorption Costing

Total Absorption Costing is the method by which all costs are listed and totalled in order to calculate the Total Cost (and thereafter a selling price) for a product or service.

Also, by accurately identifying all costs for a given period of time, you can ensure that all expenditure can be met provided that income levels are maintained at expected volumes or better. This maintenance of expected volumes of business results in the organisation or department knowing that all its costs will be covered for a planned future period (usually one year).

Example for TDC

Looking at our TDC example, we can determine a product cost by listing all known costs for that product. This summary could be tabulated to appear as follows (though a much more extensive and definitive list of costs may appear in reality):

Product A4U	Totals (£)
Direct Costs:	
Materials	4,400
Salaries – design	16,500
Salaries – delivery	6,000
Commission	1,500
Indirect Costs:	
Insurance	600
Stationery	600
Travel/subsistence	900
Telephones	1,800
Overheads	5,500
Total costs	**37,800**
Selling price	**45,000**
Surplus/profit	**7,200**

> ? Now you have a systematic way of listing your costs for a specific purpose, why not calculate an accurate cost, and selling price for each of your products or services? How healthy does your profit or surplus look?

Competitive Costing

One of the disadvantages of total absorption costing is that costs can sometimes be 'conveniently' absorbed into overheads. Often these overheads are then applied to product costs by the addition of a percentage value – that is, you may be told that "overheads (or possibly a 'management' charge) will be applied to all products as an addition of 30% on direct costs".

In fact, mis-applying costs into the Overhead category, coupled with the application of 'across-the-board' percentages, can lead to some products or services subsidising others that are not producing any actual surplus or contribution to the organisation. For this reason it is important that you analyse costs as effectively and accurately as possible so that you can define the real contribution made to the organisation of every different product or service on offer.

Just how important this is can be shown by the example of a small business client who was concerned that his business seemed to be working harder yet producing less profit. He had a product range of around one hundred, small-value consumer items, some of which were purchased together by customers. When I asked if he knew what the profit margin was on each product item, he responded, "I don't have time for that!" However, once the costs were calculated on the basis given in this chapter it quickly became obvious that around 40 per cent of the products were loss-making – my client was working harder to give money to customers!

The method I would recommend to you when you are looking *competitively* at your product/service costs, is to investigate all indirect costs in detail to ascertain if they can be allocated directly to a product/service rather than being assumed to be a part of overheads.

Cost apportionment

When you start looking at your costs in detail, you will probably find that some of them cover more than one function – for example, the head chef in a restaurant who supervises other kitchen staff as well as cooks meals.

This deeper analysis of cost focus is equally important when trying to identify the real focus of overheads. An example would be when trying to decide how to apportion the rent for premises between the different functions that occupy those premises.

The methods used for apportionment can be divided into three categories – costs related to space (e.g. premises), capacity (e.g. machinery and equipment) and time (e.g. staff).

Example for TDC

Going back to the TDC example used earlier, we can now provide a revised product cost based on competitive costing:

Product A4U	Totals (£)
Direct Costs:	
Materials	4,400
Salaries – design	16.500
Salaries – delivery	6,000
Commission	1,500
Indirect Costs:	
Insurance	100
Stationery	250
Travel/subsistence	1,150
Telephones	650
Overheads	3,700
Total costs	**34,250**
Selling price	**45,000**
Surplus/profit	**10,750**

As you can see from the TDC example, this product now shows a lower overall cost that would enable the company to reduce the selling price while maintaining a good profit level, or keep the selling price and increase the profit level. However, in reality using a basic total absorption costing system resulted in this A4U product subsidising other products by £3,550, or around 10% of the total costs. In turn, this probably means that TDC was selling another product that was actually making a loss!

> **?** Do you think that your costs and overheads may have been calculated in the past in any way other than that described above? If so, perhaps this is a good time to re-visit all of your cost calculations, and re-calculate them to make sure that your products/services show the level of contribution that you think they do.

Once costs have been apportioned and calculated using the methods recommended above, your organisation will know which products or services are producing an appropriate level of contribution and you can check prices against competitors to determine the products that you are producing most effectively. Increasing the sale of those products then increases your profitability in relation to effort!

When you know that you have a range of cost-effective products, you can complete the financial requirements of your organisation's business plan by producing financial projections, or budgets, for the foreseeable future.

Budgeting

A budget is a plan outlining the expected total costs of providing a specified level of products or services. It will say, "If the organisation is to produce a total output of £xxx, we will require £xx to cover the costs involved".

A budget is usually drawn up using experiences of the past combined with a forecast for the future – its aim is to ensure the best possible use of resources to achieve given objectives.

Clearly, if people are to be measured against the objectives in a budget, those employees should positively contribute to the formulation of the budget.

? Does your organisation have budgets at the moment? If so, who sets them? Do people in different parts of the organisation contribute to how budgets are made up originally? Do you think that your budgeting system is effective?

Areas covered by your budget will depend on the products or services you produce, but are likely to include:

- the number of product units that contribute to total revenue (in a public sector organisation this figure may be number of patients, number of taxable households, or details of the caseload to be undertaken by the organisation)

- the income or value that will flow into the organisation from those units (or from direct grants in a public sector organisation)

- the cost of materials needed to produce that level of output

- the wages, salaries, social benefit payments, etc. of all the people contributing to the work

- the cost of running the equipment resources needed to produce and support the work (e.g. lighting; power; stationery; telephones etc.)

- the cost of providing and maintaining the place

of work (eg. rent; rates; insurance; cleaning etc.)

- the cost of support services (e.g. personnel; medical; accounting; administration; security; etc.)

So, a budget is a summary of future costs and income.

You might assume that trying to predict a future budget can only result from a series of 'guesstimates'. However, you have already seen how product costs can be recorded and you may have your lists of costs ready to produce your budget. Hopefully, you have also recognised that if the organisation is to be managed viably the figures must be as accurate as possible.

Your plan must also try to address future financial pressures that were not readily observable at the time that products were costed. The overall business plan should reflect the cost of future opportunities to expand operations, or move into new operational areas, while at the same time focusing on issues that could lead to rising costs, and/or difficulties in increasing income to cover existing patterns of costs.

Budgeting techniques

Budgets are usually prepared using one of three techniques:

- Incremental budgeting
- Zero-based budgeting
- Flexed budgeting*

---

* For more detailed information on budgeting, please refer to the Easy Step by Step Guide to Better Budgeting for Your Business.

Incremental Budgeting

When one year's budget is based on the previous year's expenditure, there is no incentive for anyone to save money on their budgets. The more they spend one year, the more they will have available to spend the next.

An even worse scenario can be that budgets based on incremental additions can quickly produce uncontrolled costs, to a point where it becomes cheaper for the organisation to buy in a whole department's services from an external provider, thereby leading to the redundancy of the department!

Looking at the operation as a whole, an organisation can be forced out of business as a result of its inability to maintain prices below those of other competitive organisations.

> The aim of a budget
> is to make the most effective use
> of available resources
> in order to achieve objectives

To achieve the best performance from your organisation, it is important that every purchase is undertaken in the most cost-effective way. This means that you must examine each purchase on the basis of **value-for-money**. Adopting this approach may involve:

- negotiating the same level and quality of goods/ services at a more advantageous price

- securing an increased level/quality of goods/ services for the same expenditure.

I bet this is what you would like to happen in your

organisation? Well, the system for achieving this value-for-money analysis is known as Zero-based budgeting.

Zero-based budgeting

As its name implies, this system of budgeting starts from the assumption of a **nil** or **zero base**.

With the zero-base in mind, you question every item of expenditure in order to:

1 determine that the purchase is absolutely necessary

2 investigate how that purchase could be obtained in the most cost-effective way.

There is, of course, a need to take into account anticipated increases in prices due to inflation, but even here this should be done on an item-by-item basis rather than as a coverall percentage increase.

Since, under a zero-base system, you assure yourself that every item of expenditure is necessary and is being obtained in the most cost-effective way, you may have realised that this technique also prevents you from building in a 'little extra amount for a rainy day' – i.e. some additional cost to cover items you had not thought about.

> **?** Is this idea of a hidden 'nest egg' an issue for you? Do you include some hidden allowances in your budgets, or is it common practice in your organisation? What are the advantages and disadvantages of having this hidden extra? How do you think it could be dealt with constructively?

To many managers, this hidden 'nest egg' is an important part of the budgeting process, and we all know that events do occur that cannot be predicted and/or are out of a manager's hands to influence.

What you need is some way of allowing for these 'unknown contingencies' to cover emergencies that might arise at some point through the life of the budget period.

The size of a contingency allowance should be related to:

• the overall size of the total budget

• the type of function carried out by the working unit.

The work of some functions, and therefore their costs, will not change from day to day irrespective of perhaps quite dramatic changes going on around. Other functions may be directly involved in those dramatic changes and may therefore need extra resources to deal with them.

For example, a stable function such as accounting should require a very small (if any) contingency allowance, whereas a Public Relations operation that has to respond to unusual events could need a substantial contingency allowance.

You may well question how you can possibly know about unknown emergencies that might arise in the future. In fact, most emergencies tend to be the culmination of events that have started much earlier, or are events repeated from the past. With some attention it may be possible to identify *now* the development of factors that you will call emergencies in the future. However, most organisations have no system for recording the factors that create such emergencies and therefore fail to identify the opportunities to plan for the future.

> **?** Do you have any system for recording the day-to-day occurrences that you didn't expect or allow for? Have you had the experience of thinking, "that happened last year and I forgot all about it"?

Planning to avoid as many 'emergencies' as possible, needs an emergency-planning tool. I call this tool a **budget journal**.

Keeping a budget journal

To illustrate the origin and use of the budget journal, I will recount a little of my personal history and experience.

I originated the idea of a budget journal some years ago when, as a budget-responsible senior manager, I found that unexpected events severely influenced my department's ability to maintain its budgets. The organisation operated in London, in the field of private medicine with budgets calculated according to the number of patient appointments that could be filled during each working day.

Early in my first year of responsibility (previous budgets had been poorly calculated and maintained), industrial action by London Underground personnel resulted in prospective patients not being able to get to our central London location. Underground trains did not run, buses were crowded and late, taxis were virtually unobtainable, and roads were jammed with people trying to keep appointments throughout the city. The result was that revenues for the duration of the strike were substantially reduced, to the point that they could not be retrieved during the remainder of the budgeted year.

During a subsequent discussion, I found that long-term staff were well aware that in previous years, a London Underground strike had occurred more often than not at a similar time of year. The reason for this cyclical event was that wage negotiations usually began at a similar time of year and invariably broke down when the parties could not agree. The result was industrial action as a run-up to eventual agreement.

However, this course of events had not been remembered or mentioned to me when I prepared my budgets. During that first year a number of other unexpected (to me) events occurred, some repeated and others for the first time.

In order to prevent any future oversight of a past event, I started a budget journal in which I, and other members of staff, recorded *every* event that had not been foreseen and built into our budgets. When the next round of budget planning took place, the budget journal was our first port of call, with us investigating all the entries to make sure that we included in our budget planning any previously forgotten events.

Because investigation of the budget journal was the first process in the preparation of all subsequent budgets, the result was that predicted accuracy was maintained at a very high level, without the use of contingency allowances.

> **?** Would a budget journal be a useful tool for you to adopt for your organisation? If so, perhaps this is a good time to start one and to write into it as many of the unexpected events of the past year that you can remember. Why not get other members of your staff to do the same?

Finally, it is vital for your organisation that everyone understands and avoids the dangers presented by contingency allowances. It is human nature for a manager to try to 'play it safe' by inserting an over-large contingency allowance in his/her budgets.

Indeed, in some organisations this practice is positively encouraged by initial budgets being systematically cut without any valid reason. Managers get to know that whatever their budgets say, the 'boss' or the finance department will always reduce it with little reference to the problems this might cause the manager in trying to effectively manage his/her department with less money.

> Budgets over-inflated by projected contingency costs, and budgets 'chopped' indiscriminately, both lead to the same result – an organisation unable to be optimally effective and competitive.

It is therefore extremely important that you ensure that if contingency allowances are used in your organisation, they are well-founded and limited to very minor amounts in relation to the total budget.

Flexed budgeting

Unfortunately, organisations are not always most supportive when the budgeting process is implemented. A further barrier to effective budgeting is that, when preparing budgets for your business plan, you might feel the need to be 'safe rather than sorry' – to submit a relatively safe budget that you can achieve with relative ease.

> **?** Is this something you have done in the past or perhaps consider is reasonable for your organisation? What do you think are the advantages and disadvantages of 'safe' budgets? If you have subordinates that submit budgets to you, do you think that they might submit 'safe' budgets? How does that make you feel?

The question that you perhaps need to ask yourself is, 'Is it better to aim at 20% and achieve 25%, or to aim at 30% and achieve 28%?' In many organisations a manager in the first case would be praised and the second one reprimanded.

This type of situation is more likely to occur if performance in your organisation is measured against specific budget outcomes, upon which a bonus or promotion might depend.

However, by adopting this route you are failing to present to decision-makers all the information available, yet expecting them to make the best decisions. From a business planning point of view, this could be disastrous. Adopting a 'safe budgeting' process then removes the opportunity for your organisation to make competitive decisions that could improve its position in the marketplace.

> ?It is better to aim at 25 per cent improvement in performance and miss it by a couple of points, than to aim at 15 per cent improvement and better it by a couple of points!

In order to provide a safety net for yourself and other managers, yet also provide the maximum amount of information in your business plan on which to base business decisions, you can 'flex' your budgets to show;

- the most likely achievable results

- the most pessimistic alternative results

- the most optimistic alternative results.

A flexed budgeting technique also gives you scope to aim at your most optimistic targets without the risk of 'blame' if you don't quite achieve them.

What you would be saying is, "I am pretty sure I can make the achievable budget, but have shown what the worst scenario could be. With support I am also very willing to aim for the highest possible achievement!"

For example, a Flexed Budget for TDC is shown on the next page. In this example:

- inflation has been calculated at a highest value of 15%, an expected value of 10% or a lowest value of 5%

- the increase in business has been calculated at a worst outcome of 5%, an expected 10%, or a best outcome of 20%

- all items have been increased by the percentage increases for inflation and additional business.

As you can see from the budget on page 86, the business plan can target a best estimate (most likely achievable) surplus/profit of £6,300 compared with a previous year of £3,500, provided everything goes to plan. If predicted potential problems arise, it will achieve a loss of £250, but with the extra effort (and perhaps some extra investment) it could aim at making £9,125.

The organisation can now decide how it will address the three options provided by the business plan, and what level of support it is willing to provide in order to achieve the required outcome.*

---

* For more information on budgeting and budgetary control, see the Easy Step by Step Guide to Better Budgeting for Your Business.

£000's	Last year	BEST ESTIMATE Inflation at 10%	Increase 10%	TARGET BUDGET	FLEXED MINIMUM Inflation 15%	Increase 5%	MIN BUDGET	FLEXED MAXIMUM Inflation 5%	Increase 20%	MAX BUDGET
Income:										
Product A4U	950	95	95	1,140	143	48	1,140	48	190	1,188
Product B4U	610	61	61	732	92	31	732	31	122	763
Product C4U	240	24	24	288	36	12	288	12	48	300
TOTAL	**1,800**	**180**	**180**	**2,160**	**271**	**91**	**2,160**	**91**	**360**	**2,251**
Direct Costs:										
Materials	176	18	18	211	26	9	211	9	35	220
Salaries – design	330	33	33	396	50	17	396	17	66	413
Salaries – delivery	240	24	24	288	36	12	288	12	48	300
Commission	60	6	6	72	9	3	72	3	12	75
Indirect Costs:										
Insurance	4	0	0	5	1	0	5	0	1	5
Stationery	10	1	1	12	2	1	12	1	2	13
Travel/subsistence	46	5	5	55	7	2	55	2	9	58
Telephones	26	3	3	31	4	1	31	1	5	33
Overheads	148	15	15	178	22	7	178	7	30	185
TOTAL COSTS	**1,040**	**104**	**104**	**1,248**	**156**	**52**	**1,248**	**52**	**208**	**1,300**
SURPLUS/PROFIT	**760**			**912**			**912**			**950**

In summary

In this chapter we have looked at the issues of financing the business plan. In particular we have identified the importance of the following:

- competitively costing your products using cost apportionment effectively

- including in your business plan an effective budget, which will probably be based on a zero-based budgeting technique

- avoiding excessive contingency costs by using a budget journal

- including in your business plan a flexed budget for the coming year, thereby providing maximum information to decision-makers on the opportunities available to the organisation in different business environments.

We have now looked at all the 'planks' that you will need to put in place to achieve your business planning objectives.

It is now time to put all the information together to complete a business plan that can be submitted to the most senior panel of your organisation, and can also be used to support submissions for raising finance for expansion.

9

Making it happen!

At the beginning of this book, I defined the business plan as a document with the following characteristics:

- being produced now

- explaining a projected future

- detailing the relative position of different commercial factors

- showing how those parts will combine to produce the planned future.

> **A business plan is a schedule of factors brought together to create a desired future**

Throughout the book, I have encouraged you to think about your organisation and write down relevant information for inclusion in your business plan.

Therefore, you should now have a good part of your

plan already written, albeit in note form. The details you should have are as follows:

- A SWOT analysis that you began while reading Chapter 2 and have probably reviewed and updated as you have proceeded through this book – it should now be pretty accurate!

- SMART objectives for at least the coming year. You may have them detailed as Mission, Goals and Values but whatever you call them they should meet the SMART criteria. You should also have considered how 'balanced' the objectives are in the terms explained in Chapter 3.

- A review of your products or services with particular emphasis on any changes you might need to make in order to meet current or future market demands (Chapter 4).

- A market research report that tells you how your products are currently placed in the marketplace, and the possible future demands of your customers (Chapter 4).

- A customer analysis detailing who your customers are, how loyal they are likely to be and how their future requirements could impact on your business (Chapter 5).

- A competitor analysis showing the position of your competitors in relation to your current business, and how competitor activity might impact on your business in the future (Chapter 5).

- A promotion plan to support the planned future growth of the business (Chapter 6).

- A review of the distribution channels that you use and any recommendations for change and improvement (Chapter 6).

- An assessment of the people in your organisation and your plan for getting and retaining the right people, and providing training to support your business plan (Chapter 7).

- A competitive cost analysis for your products or services (Chapter 8).

- A financial analysis of the business and a flexed budget for the lifetime of your business plan (Chapter 8).

Remember, any changes that you propose in your plan will need to be considered in relation to all the other factors in the plan, and particularly to the costs that will be attracted by those changes. For example, if you plan to take on more staff or to introduce new products, your plan would need to give a detailed summary of the training necessary for staff to achieve an acceptable level of performance, and should show the cost of recruiting and training these personnel.

Revisiting the planning diagram shown again below, introduced in chapter 3, you will now understand that the factors listed above are the action steps that are necessary to bridge the gap between the current position and the desired future position.

You are also hopefully aware of the consequences of failing to adequately cover those steps, and of the commercial sharks waiting if you fall through the gap that would be left by a missing step!

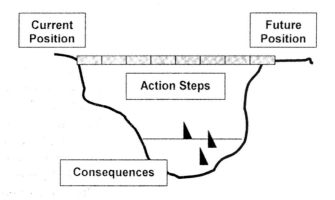

As explained in Chapter 2, the process illustrated in this diagram is the following:

* the movement from where you are now, to where you want to be – that is, the 'sun, moon and stars' of your aspirations

* the *action steps* you need to put into place to enable you to bridge the gap between the present and the future

* the *consequences* that are the result of you failing to effectively plan your action steps, or leaving a gap in the bridge. This leaves you vulnerable to falling into the shark-infested waters below!

Managing the plan

Because of the amount of time and attention you have paid to it, your current business plan is probably the most detailed and accurate assessment of the business that you have ever achieved. You now know where you want to go, how you can get there, and the barriers you may have to overcome on the way.

Your plan will probably be for one year, though there may be aspects of it that will extend to a longer period.

However, the most important time aspect in making your plan work is not the longer term but the short term. From the point at which you complete and issue the plan the clock is ticking! Every day that goes by without some action towards achieving the planning outcomes is a day wasted and a time that you cannot make up again. Therefore, you need to include in your plan not only what you aim to achieve during the year (or longer period of the plan), but also the stages of achievement that should be reached over much shorter periods, possibly of one month duration!

Your plan needs to say, 'By the end of month 1 these are the actions that should have been completed, and these are the expected costs. Therefore, your plan must include an action schedule that shows the activities that must be completed by a specific time in order for your plan to succeed.

For example, the table below is an activity schedule showing the following information for TDC:

- the level of sales income the organisation expects to achieve from existing business, for each month, according to any seasonal effects applied to their products
- the process for developing new courses, with target dates when each stage should be completed
- the date when the courses are packaged and ready for distribution (end-March)
- the date when the new courses are promoted in the marketplace (beginning of April)

ACTION PLAN – SALES (£000's)	Jan	Feb	Mch	Apr	May	Jun	Jul	Aug	Sep
Existing Sales	£	£	£	£	£	£	£	£	£
New product development:									
Development seminar	x								
Outline course writing		x	x						
Editing and re-writing			x						
Packaging for distribution			x						
Promotion of new courses				x					
New Sales					£	£	£	£	£
TOTAL TARGET SALES £	£	£	£	££	££	££	££	££	

- the expected sales income from new courses from the beginning of May

- the total sales targets for the year, by month.

As you have probably realised, this schedule provides a clear outline to managers when activities have to be completed by in order to meet the organisation's objectives.

Of course, the business plan should contain an activity schedule for every activity, specifically detailing all new activities that are vital to success. For example, the need for more staff at some point during the year would have an activity schedule for recruitment, appointment dates (bearing in mind the need for new staff to complete resignation contract times), training time, and job lead-in time.

Also, and most importantly, all activity schedules should be linked to a seasonalised financial budget covering all targeted income and costs for the period. Seasonalisation will depend on the type of industry in which you operate, but could include the following:

- budgets based on the number of *working* days in each month, where output or income is affected by the number of days available

- budgets based on product seasonalisation, for example where product sales are focused on Christmas or other holiday periods

- budgets based on large-scale projects that are focused on specific dates through the year (or longer)

- budgets based on mass payments, such as the receipt of tax payments by local municipal authorities at a specific time of year.

Also, once seasonalised budgets have been set, they will need to be managed and controlled with equal vigour to the control of all other activity schedules.*

It is this level of control that makes business planning successful.

However, there is one further aspect of business planning that you will certainly want to explore at some time. If an opportunity arises after you have formulated your business plan, must you ignore it because you have already planned your future, or can you embrace it enthusiastically?

Changing the plan

Let's be clear. A business plan is not set in concrete!

However, bear in mind that you have probably sweated blood and tears over a fair period of time in order to formulate a plan that covers the following criteria:

- meets all the aspects of the SWOT analysis that you started with

- puts into place all the planks to get you from where you are now, to where you want to be in the future.

Therefore, while your business plan is not set in concrete, it is also not some thing that should be swept aside without a great deal of thought.

You have seen that, in formulating your plan, you determined all the factors that would help you to

---

* See the Easy Step by Step Guide to Better Budgeting for Your Business.

achieve, and that might stand in the way of the future to which you aspire.

Therefore, any opportunity, or disaster or major change to your plan or its projected outcomes, must be considered with the same intensity that you have given to formulating your plan in the first place.

So, a change that you want to consider should go through all the stages that your plan went through:

A review of your SWOT analysis to determine the strengths and weaknesses that the change may bring into focus.

- A review of your SMART to determine how the change will help you to achieve them, both now and in the long term. If the change is outside the current objectives, you may need to start again from the beginning to change the objectives and completely redesign your business plan!

- A review of how the change might affect your products or services with particular emphasis on meeting current or future market demands.

- A market research report that tells you how the change you are considering will meet the needs of the Marketplace, and particularly the needs of your customers.

- A customer analysis to determine how the proposed change will influence the products and services you offer to customers.

- A competitor analysis showing the competitor advantage you are likely to gain from the proposed change.

- A promotion plan to support the proposed change.

- A review of distribution channels to determine how they might be affected by the proposed change.

- An assessment of how the proposed change might impact on the people in your organisation and your plan for addressing any factors identified.

- A competitive cost analysis related to the proposed change – how much will it cost and what financial benefits could it bring?

- A financial analysis of the business, including all the costs related to the proposed change, and a flexed budget for the lifetime of a revised business plan.

This may seem a formidable task to carry out and it is probably worth repeating my advice from the beginning of this book:

> It is not a sin when things do not go according to plan.
>
> *It is a sin not to know* when things are not working to plan.

If you don't properly plan for the proposed change, you are not going to know whether the change is working or not!

So, whenever something arises that is outside your business plan, perhaps the question you should ask yourself first is, 'Is the proposed change worth the effort required to go through the process detailed in this section?' If the answer is, 'No!' then the proposed change is probably a red herring (even if it is a tempting one) and likely to cause more trouble than it is worth.

A change that is worthwhile to your business is worth the effort of making a proper assessment!

In summary

In this chapter we have considered the following aspects of business planning:

- what makes a good business plan?
- how to manage a business plan
- how to manage the changes proposed in the business plan
- how and when to change a business plan.

You are now in a position to create and manage an effective and successful business plan.

Business planning is an effort-intensive process but one that is likely to provide you with a number of benefits, including the following:

- it gives you a great deal of insight into your organisation that you probably could not have achieved otherwise
- it can bring together all the people in the organisation, and particularly the key personnel
- it provides information for potential investors that will give them the confidence to provide finance or investment for organisation growth
- it provides a sound management tool that greatly enhances the probability of success

- it substantially reduces the possibility of panic management and management fire-fighting, and therefore reduces the number of sleepless nights for you!

As a business consultant, I always feel that a good business plan is a gift for everyone. Therefore, it is worth doing, and it is worth doing properly!

> **Here's to your sound business management!**